The Ultimate Mythology Quiz

G000068216

B.R. Egginton

Contents

Prologue...3

Questions (Easy)..6

Questions (Average) 33

Questions (Expert) 53

Answers 65

Prologue

'The Bible has noble poetry in it... and some good morals and a wealth
of obscenity, and upwards of a thousand lies.'
Mark Twain

'I believe in everything until it's disproved. So I believe in fairies, the
myths, dragons. It all exists, even if it's in your mind. Who's to say that
dreams and nightmares aren't as real as the here and now?'
John Lennon

How did the Earth, the Sun, the Moon and the stars come into being?
Where do we come from, and where do we go when we die? What
causes thunder and lightning, and why are there droughts and floods?

These are just a few questions mankind has asked itself since the birth
of civilisation, and the stories that have been told over the aeons to
answer these queries – from the inventive to the downright
unbelievable – have come together under one broad church: uniting the
world as one.

That broad church is mythology.

The study of mythology began in ancient times. Rival classes of the
Greek myths by Euhemerus, Plato and Sallustius were developed by the
Neoplatonists and later revived by Renaissance mythographers.

Today, the study of mythology continues to flourish in a wide variety
of academic fields, including folklore studies, philology, psychology
and anthropology.

And then there's the most thrilling discipline of all – trivia.

This book contains mythological trivia from every corner of the Earth
and is divided into three levels of difficulty: easy (with multiple
choice), average and expert.

So regardless of whether you're new to the study of mythology or consider yourself a mythology buff, this is the quiz book for you.

All that's left to say is 'life is a conundrum of esoterica'. And for that we should be thankful. Because if we had all the answers, life – robbed of adventures and dreams – would be about as interesting as watching paint dry.

Questions

Easy 1

Q1 (South American) What is the mythical city of El Dorado most commonly associated with?

A Longevity
B Wealth
C Literature
D Gods

Q2 (Japanese) The Eight Thunders are guardians of what?

A Sea
B Japanese people
C Emperor
D Underworld

Q3 (Inuit) Who is the boy Moon Brother's sister?

A Star Sister
B Sky Sister
C Sun Sister
D Earth Sister

Q4 (Hindu) How many heads does the creator god Brahma have?

A 1
B 2
C 3
D 4

Q5 (Persian) The goddess Anahita is associated with what planet?

A Mercury
B Venus
C Pluto
D Neptune

Q6 (Egyptian) Aalu, the paradise of Osiris, is located far in what direction?

A North
B South
C East
D West

Q7 (Roman) Bacchus is god of what?

A Wine
B Perfume
C Flowers
D Dancing

Q8 (Mesopotamian) Enuma Elish is the Akkadian story of what?

A Their greatest ruler
B Creation
C God's teachings
D Legendary creatures

Q9 (Siberian) Namu is a man who is said to have survived what disastrous event?

A Meteorite
B Earthquake
C Tornado
D Flood

Q10 (North American) Ababinili is the supreme god of what tribe?

A Chickasaw
B Seminole
C Creek
D Ute

Easy 2

Q1 (North American) Wakan Tanka is the creator god of what tribe?

A Pawnee
B Iroquois
C Sioux
D Cherokee

Q2 (Chinese) What creature is the Enlightener of Darkness?

A Dragon
B Fairy
C Basilisk
D Griffin

Q3 (Hebrew) In the *Book of Revelation* Abaddon was king of an army of what?

A Locusts
B Scorpions
C Wolves
D Eagles

Q4 (African) Elefo is a magic what used by the god Itonde to predict the future and foretell death?

A Stone
B Dagger
C Bell
D Mirror

Q5 (Australian) Keen Kings were a race of men with what?

A Horns
B Wings
C Claws
D Tails

Q6 (Norse) Balder was the son of what god?

A Freyr
B Thor
C Loki
D Odin

Q7 (Irish) Ale of Goibhniu conferred what on those who drank it?

A Super-strength
B Immortality
C Good fortune
D Invisibility

Q8 (Arabian) Sinbad is best known as being a what?

A Soldier
B King
C Sailor
D Inventor

Q9 (Greek) Albion was the king of what race?

A Giants
B Cyclops
C Dragons
D Demigods

Q10 (Greek) Ambrosia is a food that confers everlasting what?

A Youth
B Health
C Happiness
D Popularity

Easy 3

Q1 (Greek) *Odyssey* is an epic story by who?

A Sophocles
B Homer
C Aristotle
D Plato

Q2 (European) What was the *Nibelungenlied*?

A Religious text
B Play
C Mythical king's epitaph
D Epic poem

Q3 (Central American) Chamer was the Mayan god of what?

A Fertility
B Thunder
C Agriculture
D Death

Q4 (Thai) Thens refers to lords of what?

A Sea
B Sky
C Underworld
D Forests

Q5 (British) Gorlagon was King Arthur's pet what?

A Dragon
B Wolf
C Cat
D Snake

Q6 (Japanese) Maneko nook is a charm in the form of what animal?

A Squirrel
B Wolf
C Boar
D Cat

Q7 (Roman) Who was Romulus and Remus's father?

A Zeus
B Mars
C Hades
D Julius Caesar

Q8 (Norse) What weapon does the god Thor wield?

A Sword
B Spear
C Hammer
D Crossbow

Q9 (Greek) What colour are the Apples of the Hesperides?

A Red
B Black
C Gold
D Silver

Q10 (Greek) What do gorgons have instead of hair?

A Nothing
B Tree branches
C Snakes
D Helmets

Easy 4

Q1 (Greek) Who was the Greek sky god?

A Poseidon
B Hades
C Zeus
D Hermes

Q2 (West Indies) The Haitian goddess of love Erzulie is represented wearing how many rings?

A 1
B 2
C 3
D 4

Q3 (Cambodia) Prah Keo refers to a holy what?

A Sword
B Jewel
C Chair
D Crown

Q4 (Korean) The heaven Gamag Nara is a land of near total what?

A Peace
B Darkness
C Clouds
D Drunkenness

Q5 (European) Alberich is the king of what race?

A Ogres
B Goblins
C Dwarfs
D Nymphs

Q6 (British) Uther Pendragon's brother was killed by what warlord?

A Robin Hood
B Hereward the Wake
C Boudicca
D Vortigern

Q7 (South American) A Yaguarogin is a tiger of what colour?

A White
B Gold
C Green
D Black

Q8 (Japanese) The Shinto god Aizen-myoo is the personification of what?

A Betrayal
B Anger
C Love
D Youth

Q9 (Japanese) Kuni-toko-tachi is the god of what mountain?

A Mount Aino
B Mount Haku
C Mount Kita
D Mount Fuji

Q10 (North American) The Sioux culture hero Ikto is said to have invented what?

A Speech
B Writing
C Wheels
D Bow and arrow

Easy 5

Q1 (European) Kudai is the supreme god of what group?

A Vikings
B Saxons
C Tatars
D Slavs

Q2 (British) The Green Knight is associated with which Knight of the Round Table?

A Galahad
B Gawain
C Percival
D Lancelot

Q3 (Japanese) Ame-no-wo-ha-bari is the magic what of the god Izanagi?

A Sceptre
B Helmet
C Sword
D Glasses

Q4 (Egyptian) A person's Ba is their what?

A Heart
B Soul
C Conscience
D Blood

Q5 (Greek) What ship carried Jason and the Argonauts?

A *Mayflower*
B *Argo*
C *Titanic*
D *Victory*

Q6 (Greek) What was Daedalus's occupation?

A Explorer
B Advisor
C Mathematician
D Architect

Q7 (Central American) What shape is the Mayan sun god Ah Kin's third eye?

A Circular
B Square
C Diamond
D Triangular

Q8 (British) What did King Arthur pull the sword Excalibur out of?

A The previous King of the Britons
B A stone
C The earth
D The forge

Q9 (Egyptian) In some stories, Ra created humans with what?

A Poo
B Clay
C Tears
D Honey

Q10 (Pacific Islands) What did the Polynesian goddess Pere create?

A Flowers
B Humans
C The sea
D Lava

Easy 6

Q1 (Greek) Orpheus was given a lyre by what god?

A Hermes
B Hades
C Ares
D Apollo

Q2 (Slav) Dabog is a sun god who rides across the sky every day on what?

A Chariot
B Dragon
C Boat
D Star

Q3 (British) The Nine Ladies is a megalithic structure in what English county?

A Wiltshire
B Shropshire
C Herefordshire
D Derbyshire

Q4 (Roman) What craft is the god Vulcan associated with?

A Carpentry
B Painting
C Sculpting
D Metalwork

Q5 (Siberian) The creator god Es made humanity from what ingredient?

A Clay
B Wood
C Corn
D Soil

Q6 (Japanese) Where was Wu Kang banished to?

A Underworld
B Mainland Asia
C The moon
D A cave

Q7 (Greek) What animal was the hunter Actaeon turned into by the goddess Artemis?

A Lion
B Snake
C Rabbit
D Stag

Q8 (Greek) Dionysus is the god of what type of drink?

A Water
B Wine
C Mead
D Ambrosia

Q9 (Central American) How often is the Aztec festival Atamalqualiztli held?

A Every month
B Every 6 months
C Every year
D Every 8 years

Q10 (Inuit) The god of healing Eyeekalduk is so small he lives in a…

A Shell
B Cup
C Shoe
D Pebble

Easy 7

Q1 (British) The king Lud is said to have founded what city?

A London
B Leeds
C Lancaster
D Ludlow

Q2 (Hindu) The demon Kumbhakharma is awake for one day in every (?) months?

A 2
B 3
C 6
D 9

Q3 (African) In the lore of the Yoruba what was the first living thing to be created by the god Olorun?

A Humans
B Insects
C Palm trees
D Fish

Q4 (Australian) Wurruri is responsible for what difference between the Aboriginal tribes?

A Pallet
B Clothing
C Language
D Appearance

Q5 (Greek) A Cornucopia is a horn always full of what?

A Medicine
B Food and drink
C Blood of Hercules
D Gold

Q6 (Central American) In Aztec creation stories Quetzalcoatl was the ruler of what Sun?

A First Sun
B Second Sun
C Fourth Sun
D Fifth Sun

Q7 (British) Who raised the Knight of the Round Table, Galahad?

A Merlin
B King Arthur
C The Lady of the Lake
D Monks

Q8 (Japanese) The ho-o is the Japanese version of what mythical creature?

A Vampire
B Phoenix
C Elf
D Dragon

Q9 (Hindu) The elephant-headed god of art, Ganesha, had his head cut off by what relation?

A Father
B Mother
C Brother
D Uncle

Q10 (Egyptian) What did the god Anubis weigh?

A Hearts
B Souls
C Bodies
D Gold

Easy 8

Q1 (Japanese) The farmer Heitaro famously became fond of what type of tree?

A Pine
B Willow
C Sycamore
D Ash

Q2 (Hindu) How many sons did the king Kuvalayaswa have?

A 0
B 13
C 101
D 21,000

Q3 (Egyptian) An Ankh is a symbol of what?

A Renewal
B Death
C Life
D Change

Q4 (African) Mantis is a hero of the Khoisan who is said to have stolen what from an ostrich?

A Feathers
B Fire
C Eggs
D Gold

Q5 (Greek) The sun god Cadmus is said to have introduced what?

A The alphabet
B The Olympics
C Democracy
D Deserts

Q6 (Greek) Calliope was one of the nine what?

A Trolls
B Mermaids
C Muses
D Cupids

Q7 (British) Where was King Arthur's court based?

A Winchester
B London
C Camelot
D Gondor

Q8 (British) According to legend the Giant's Causeway in Northern Ireland was built by giants to form a road across to what country?

A Iceland
B England
C Scotland
D Wales

Q9 (Egyptian) After trapping his brother Osiris in a chest, what river did Seth throw him into?

A Niger
B Danube
C Nile
D Yellow

Q10 (African) In the lore of the Yoruba people, the god Shango lives in a palace made out of what?

A Wood
B Ice
C Brass
D Emerald

Easy 9

Q1 (Greek) What did the sirens do to lure passing sailors to sail too close to the rocks?

A Sang
B Called for help
C Littered the coast with gold
D Conjured fog

Q2 (European) Davy Jones's Locker is regarded as the grave of what?

A Dead soldiers
B Drowned seamen
C Deposed kings
D Forgotten gods

Q3 (British) The knight Balin killed what close relative with his sword?

A Father
B Mother
C Brother
D Sister

Q4 (Japanese) How many Dragon Kings are there to rule the Earth?

A 2
B 4
C 7
D 12

Q5 (Egyptian) Amen was the patron deity of what city?

A Thebes
B Alexandria
C Giza
D Memphis

Q6 (Greek) What type of powers did the Trojan princess Cassandra have?

A Telepathy
B Healing
C Prophecy
D Gold touch

Q7 (European) What type of weapon is Durindana?

A Sword
B Axe
C Spear
D Knife

Q8 (Central American) The god Quetzalcoatl is also known as the Feathered what?

A Eagle
B Serpent
C Boar
D Fox

Q9 (Hindu) The demigod Garuda was part man part what?

A Rabbit
B Lion
C Eagle
D Spider

Q10 (Norse) Einheriar are the souls of slain what?

A Livestock
B Warriors
C Children
D Monsters

Easy 10

Q1 (European) *Kalevala* is an epic story of heroes and creation, originating from what country?

A Bulgaria
B Finland
C Norway
D Germany

Q2 (Central American) Tezcatlipoca is the Aztec god of what?

A Fertility
B Sun
C Love
D War

Q3 (British) Prester John is a mythical what?

A Priest
B Sailor
C King
D Warrior

Q4 (Malay) Buttons made from the bill of a toucan are said to turn what colour when they detect poison?

A Green
B Orange
C Red
D Black

Q5 (Japanese) The warrior Hidesato famously killed a giant what?

A Worm
B Locust
C Centipede
D Moth

Q6 (Egyptian) Who is the wife of the god Osiris?

A Nut
B Isis
C Hathor
D Tefnut

Q7 (North American) In the lore of the Zuni, what happens if the Ten Corn Maidens are absent?

A Women become infertile
B A thunderstorm strikes
C Crops fail
D The world ends

Q8 (Australian) The sky god Altjira is depicted as having the feet of what bird?

A Crow
B Falcon
C Emu
D Pigeon

Q9 (Norse) What trait is the god Loki most commonly associated with?

A Strength
B Loyalty
C Vanity
D Mischief

Q10 (Greek) What is Charon's occupation?

A Mercenary
B Ferryman
C Musician
D Tailor

Easy 11

Q1 (Irish) When the warrior Finn mac Cool was born, he was thrown into the sea and emerged with what in each hand?

A Seaweed
B Eel
C Octopus
D Shells

Q2 (Arabian) How did Abdallah the Fisherman kill a sea monster?

A Poisoned the sea
B Stabbed it with a sword
C Sang
D Shouted at it

Q3 (Greek) What part of Achilles's body was vulnerable?

A Nose
B Neck
C Heart
D Heel

Q4 (Greek) After returning from killing the Minotaur, what did Theseus forget to do?

A Light a fire to signal success
B Send a letter to signal success
C Fire a cannon to signal success
D Hoist the white sail to signal success

Q5 (European) Sabra, the daughter of a pharaoh, was rescued from a dragon by what saint?

A St Patrick
B St Augustine
C St David
D St George

Q6 (Central American) Mahucutah was one of the first men in Mayan lore. How many others were there?

A 1
B 3
C 9
D 99

Q7 (British) What series of tournaments were arranged by King Arthur?

A Diamond Jousts
B Ruby Jousts
C Chivalric Jousts
D Never-ending Jousts

Q8 (British) Wayland's Smithy is a megalithic circle in what English county?

A Berkshire
B Buckinghamshire
C Kent
D Devon

Q9 (Greek) The sea god Triton assumes what form?

A Merman
B Crab
C Seagull
D Dolphin

Q10 (South American) The evil spirit Guecubu is destined to destroy the earth with what?

A A flood
B A meteorite
C An earthquake
D A poisonous cloud

Easy 12

Q1 (Irish) Uaithne refers to what magical instrument?

A Harp
B Flute
C Banjo
D Bagpipes

Q2 (Arabian) Aladdin owned a magic what?

A Quill
B Compass
C Sword
D Lamp

Q3 (Greek) What war did Achilles fight in?

A Trojan War
B Peloponnesian War
C Corinthian War
D Punic Wars

Q4 (Greek) What is Eros the god of?

A War
B Love
C Gambling
D Wind

Q5 (European) What does the Lithuanian smith god Kalvaistis make anew each day?

A Humans
B The sun
C Air
D Crops

Q6 (Central American) After the god Tezcatlipoca's foot was bitten off by a monster, what was it replaced with?

A A prosthetic foot
B A mirror
C A dagger
D A scythe

Q7 (British) The Maen Arthur, which is said to retain the imprint of the hoof of King Arthur's horse, is composed of what material?

A Gold
B Rock
C Wood
D Cotton

Q8 (Greek) Pegasus was the winged horse of what god?

A Apollo
B Hermes
C Dionysus
D Hephaestus

Q9 (Japanese) Tide Jewels are a set of jewels that give control of what?

A Daylight
B Wind
C Rainfall
D The seas

Q10 (Egyptian) The god Thoth is credited with the invention of what?

A Hieroglyphics
B Pyramids
C Papyrus
D Mummification

Average 1

Q1 (Mongolian) The warrior-hero Gesar Khan was born from what?

Q2 (East Indies) In the lore of Papua New Guinea, Oa Iriarapo was a man who made what?

Q3 (Arabian) Abou Hassan is a rich merchant in what collection of folk tales?

Q4 (Greek) Abderus served as whose armour bearer?

Q5 (Greek) Ambrosia is the food of what?

Q6 (New Zealand) Reinga was the Maori land of what?

Q7 (European) The Kraken is what kind of monster?

Q8 (Egyptian) What god travels on the solar bark?

Q9 (African) The dragon Isa Bere is said to have swallowed all the water from what river?

Q10 (Greek) The King of Athens, Aegeus, was the father of what hero?

Average 2

Q1 (New Zealand) Who was the earth-mother of the Maori?

Q2 (Central American) *Popol Vuh* is a text recounting the history of what civilisation?

Q3 (Egyptian) Which eye did the god Horus lose?

Q4 (Roman) How many faces does the god Janus have?

Q5 (Australian) Cheeroonar is a monster with the body of a man and the head of what animal?

Q6 (Greek) What goddess carries Zeus's breastplate, Aegis?

Q7 (Greek) Chiron is the king of what race?

Q8 (European) Rhine-daughters guard what in the Rhine?

Q9 (British) Who did King Arthur fall in love with?

Q10 (South American) Who did Mama Ocllo marry to found the Inca dynasty?

Average 3

Q1 (Tibetan) Da is a guardian god who sits on which shoulder?

Q2 (British) The *Historia Regum Britanniae* is a 12-volume work written in Latin by who?

Q3 (Roman) A faun is a cross between what two animals?

Q4 (Norse) Ragnarok refers to a battle that leads to what?

Q5 (Greek) Who was the father of the Minotaur?

Q6 (Greek) The Honoured Women act as gatekeepers to what?

Q7 (European) The Battle of Roncesvalles was fought between what two groups?

Q8 (British) The Holy Grail is a cup or plate that is said to have been used by who?

Q9 (Egyptian) What head does the god Anubis have?

Q10 (Egyptian) The goddess Sekhmet is commonly associated with what city?

Average 4

Q1 (Central American) Acacitli was the leader of what group?

Q2 (Buddhist) The god Acala is responsible for guarding what quarter of the world?

Q3 (British) The magician Merlin is credited with creating what table?

Q4 (Greek) Hyacinthus was a lover of what god?

Q5 (Greek) Who was Kronos's father?

Q6 (Central American) In Mayan lore, Sucunyum is the god of what?

Q7 (European) What weapon did the Roman centurion Longinus use to pierce Christ's side during the crucifixion?

Q8 (British) Some sources claim that Stonehenge was originally from what island?

Q9 (South American) Ono pacakoti was a flood sent by what Inca creator god?

Q10 (Hindu) The god Shiva was born from what part of the god Vishnu's body?

Average 5

Q1 (Greek) As well as being his wife, how was Zeus related to Hera?

Q2 (British) Goon Desert was the brother of what king?

Q3 (Korean) Gin-sai is a fabulous bird, so evil its mere shadow can do what?

Q4 (South American) Who is the Inca sun god?

Q5 (Arabian) Morgiana was whose slave in the *Arabian Nights' Entertainments*?

Q6 (North American) The lumberjack Paul Bunyan is said to have created what geographical landmark with his giant axe?

Q7 (Norse) What monster did the warrior Beowulf kill?

Q8 (Greek) Who was Daedalus's son?

Q9 (European) Kralj Matjaz was the king of what group?

Q10 (British) After being slain, the stoorworm's body became what island nation?

Average 6

Q1 (British) Which Knight of the Round Table did the Lady of the Lake raise?

Q2 (Hindu) Amrita is the what of the gods?

Q3 (Greek) The Garden of the Hesperides is the garden of what goddess?

Q4 (Greek) The son of King Minos, Glaucus, was drowned in a jar of what?

Q5 (European) The Finnish hero Ilmarinen is said to have taught humans what skill?

Q6 (British) The Perilous Seat was a place at the Round Table, reserved for the knight worthy of what?

Q7 (Egyptian) Who is the twin sister of the god Geb?

Q8 (Egyptian) What is Ra the god of?

Q9 (Roman) What is Neptune the god of?

Q10 (Mesopotamian) The king of Kish, Etana, flew to Heaven on the back of what animal?

Average 7

Q1 (European) The demon Abigor is one of the 72 Spirits of what?

Q2 (South American) Viracocha is a creator god of what people?

Q3 (Hindu) Kalpa refers to a day in the life of what god?

Q4 (Pacific Islands) The Fijian god Rokola is skilled in what craft?

Q5 (Greek) Who sliced through the Gordian knot with his sword?

Q6 (European) The Finnish magician-hero Vainamoinen is credited with the invention of what?

Q7 (Central American) What is the Aztec land of the dead called?

Q8 (British) What magician foretold Tom Thumb would be no bigger than his thumb?

Q9 (Egyptian) Hapy is a fertility god associated with what river?

Q10 (Roman) Numa Pompilius was the second king of what city state?

Average 8

Q1 (Central American) Who is the Aztec rain god?

Q2 (Buddhist) What are torn apart by dogs in Bad Dog Village?

Q3 (Egyptian) The god Horus lost an eye in a battle with what other god?

Q4 (Chinese) The philosopher Lao-tzu is the founder of what?

Q5 (Greek) Artemis is the goddess of what?

Q6 (Japanese) The Shinto sun goddess Amaterasu was produced from what part of the god Izanagi's body?

Q7 (Hindu) Which god did the demigod Garuda carry on his daily journey across the sky?

Q8 (Egyptian) What head does the goddess Nekhbet have?

Q9 (Mesopotamian) The fish god Enki rose from the waters of what gulf?

Q10 (Pacific Islands) Flaming Teeth is a giant from what island?

Average 9

Q1 (Japanese) Eater of Dreams is one of the Seven Gods of what?

Q2 (Roman) Who is said to have founded Rome?

Q3 (Pacific Islands) On the Solomon Islands, Ii'oa are the spirits of dead what?

Q4 (Chinese) The parasol tree is the only tree that what type of creature will land on?

Q5 (African) In the lore of the Hittite people, Telipinu is the god of what?

Q6 (Irish) A Gan-Ceann refers to a fairy or spirit missing what part of their anatomy?

Q7 (Greek) In what form did the goddess Athena emerge when she was born?

Q8 (Greek) Heracles killed the musician Linus with what instrument?

Q9 (British) The Fisher King was charged with keeping what?

Q10 (European) Wayland is the god of what?

Average 10

Q1 (European) Navky refers to the souls of children who died before what?

Q2 (Japanese) Why was the Shinto god of fortune, Hiru-ko, abandoned by his parents?

Q3 (Roman) What power did Apollo give Sibyl of Cumae?

Q4 (Pacific Islands) The child Dudugera was born from what part of his mother's body?

Q5 (Greek) When the Titans lost their war against the Olympians, what fate was Atlas condemned to?

Q6 (Greek) Who is the messenger of the gods?

Q7 (European) What do Firedrakes typically guard?

Q8 (British) Who was King Arthur's father?

Q9 (Hindu) How did Priyavrata create the seven continents?

Q10 (Persian) What type of monster is a Gandarewa?

Average 11

Q1 (Irish) The king of the fairies, Iubdan, possessed a pair of shoes that enabled him to travel on what?

Q2 (Arabian) The sultan, Shahriyah, in *Arabian Nights' Entertainments* killed each of his wives on what night?

Q3 (Greek) What did Narcissus fall in love with?

Q4 (European) In Germanic lore, what was the name of the dwarf who raised Siegfried?

Q5 (British) The Knight of the Round Table Agravain was killed by what other Knight of the Round Table?

Q6 (Greek) Which King of Athens accepted Theseus as his own son?

Q7 (South American) The Arawak hunter-hero Okonorote dug a hole through the floor of what?

Q8 (Hindu) What secret weapon did the gods use to kill the demon Jalandhara?

Q9 (Egyptian) What is Mahaf's job in the underworld?

Q10 (Greek) The Argonauts sailed with Jason to recover what?

Average 12

Q1 (Arabian) Who did the princess Badr al-Budur marry in the *Arabian Nights' Entertainments*?

Q2 (Greek) What river did Achillies's mother dip him in?

Q3 (Greek) The Trojan War was fought between what two groups?

Q4 (Central American) What is Xibalba in Mayan lore?

Q5 (British) The poet Thomas the Rhymer claimed to possess what power?

Q6 (Greek) The Pillars of Hercules were set at the entrance to what sea?

Q7 (Hindu) What does the monster Kabandha have on its stomach?

Q8 (Persian) What was the king Kay Kaus blinded with?

Q9 (Egyptian) Edjo is the cobra goddess of what kingdom?

Q10 (Egyptian) The goddess Nut and who else were locked together when they were born?

Average 13

Q1 (British) What relation did the Knight of the Round Table, Gaheris, kill?

Q2 (Japanese) The painter Kanasoka drew a picture of a horse so realistic that what happened?

Q3 (Roman) What is Vulcan the god of?

Q4 (Greek) Everything King Midas touched turned into what?

Q5 (Pacific Islands) Pele is the volcano goddess of what group of islands?

Q6 (North American) The young Tewa man Deerhunter was celebrated for his skill at what?

Q7 (North American) Little Man, a hero of the Metis nation, is said to own a magical what?

Q8 (Chinese) Where do the Ten Yama Kings have their courts?

Q9 (Hebrew) The serpent Leviathan is said to emit a light even brighter than what?

Q10 (Australian) What was the hunter Wyungare created from?

Average 14

Q1 (Egyptian) As well as being his wife, how is Isis related to Osiris?

Q2 (Roman) Numitor was the grandfather of what famous twins?

Q3 (Greek) The husband of Helen of Troy, Menelaus, was King of what?

Q4 (Mesopotamian) Who were sacrificed to the Ammonite god Moloch?

Q5 (Pacific Islands) The god Ndauthina is regarded as the guardian of what group?

Q6 (North American) What is the name of the turtle in Seneca lore that carries the world on its back?

Q7 (North American) In some Native American tribes the Raft of Four Sticks symbolises the four quarters of what?

Q8 (Chinese) The monk Tripitaka travelled from China to what country to obtain the Buddhist scriptures?

Q9 (African) What is notable about the feet of the Ashanti forest monster, Sasabonsam?

Q10 (Greek) Hector led the defence of what city?

Average 15

Q1 (Roman) The god Mercury is depicted wearing winged what?

Q2 (Greek) What can gorgons turn people into?

Q3 (Greek) What name was given to the daughters of Zeus and Mnemosyne?

Q4 (Hindu) How many heads does the demon Ravana have?

Q5 (North American) In Navajo lore, Atse Estsan and Atse Hastin – the first woman and first man – were created by the gods from what?

Q6 (North American) In the lore of the Chiricahua Apache, Gahe are supernatural beings that live inside what?

Q7 (Chinese) Ho Hsien-ku was one of the Eight what?

Q8 (Chinese) T'ai Shan refers to a sacred what?

Q9 (Australian) In the lore of the Aborigines, Wagu and Biljata established the rules of what?

Q10 (Greek) The god Helius drives his sun-chariot across the sky every day in what direction?

Average 16

Q1 (Greek) Tartarus is part of what realm?

Q2 (Greek) Oceanids was a river said to encircle what?

Q3 (Central American) Who is the mother of the Aztec god Huitzilopochtli?

Q4 (North American) Napi is the creator god of what tribe?

Q5 (Greek) The Thracian nymph Eurydice died after being bitten by what animal?

Q6 (Norse) The god of wisdom, Kvasir, was created from what?

Q7 (Roman) Cupid is the god of what?

Q8 (Greek) How did the king Odysseus try to avoid serving in the Trojan War?

Q9 (Norse) Who is the Norse god of thunder?

Q10 (Irish) Undry refers to a magic what?

Average 17

Q1 (Greek) The Shirt of Nessus was sent from Deianera to who?

Q2 (British) Who assumed the name Pendragon after becoming king?

Q3 (Central American) Who was the Mayan god of fertility and rain?

Q4 (Greek) The goddess Aphrodite's chariot is drawn by eight what?

Q5 (Greek) The Labours of Hercules were a series of tasks given to Hercules after he killed who?

Q6 (Norse) Managarm was one of three wolves who chase what two things?

Q7 (Siberian) What does the demon Abassylar devour?

Q8 (Greek) What creature was the son of Poseidon, Polyphemus?

Q9 (Norse) The war god Tyr had his hand bitten off by what animal?

Q10 (Greek) Who is the wife of the god Poseidon?

Average 18

Q1 (Greek) The Cypriot king Pygmalion was skilled at making what?

Q2 (Central American) In Aztec lore, how did the giant Xelhua survive the Flood?

Q3 (European) Wild Hunt refers to a noisy phantom host who rides through the sky on the back of what animal?

Q4 (Greek) Ares is the god of what?

Q5 (Norse) What instrument was the god Bragi given by dwarfs?

Q6 (Norse) Who is the principal wife of Odin?

Q7 (North American) Rabbit Boy is a hero of what Native American tribe?

Q8 (Greek) What goddess turned Medusa into a gorgon?

Q9 (Norse) The giant Vafthruthnir is best known for what trait?

Q10 (Greek) Balios was a horse, given to who by Zeus or Poseidon?

Average 19

Q1 (Greek) The nymph Oenone was abandoned by her husband in favour of who?

Q2 (Central American) Who is the patron god of the Aztecs?

Q3 (North American) What did the god Chinigchinich most notably create?

Q4 (Greek) How many eyes do cyclops have?

Q5 (Norse) Gleipnir is magic what, used to restrain the wolf Fenris?

Q6 (Norse) The fire giant Surtur is armed with what weapon?

Q7 (Chinese) The Eighteen Arhats were disciples of who?

Q8 (Greek) The satyr Marsyas is associated with what instrument?

Q9 (Australian) Bahloo is a god of what?

Q10 (Greek) How many daughters did the king Danaus have?

Average 20

Q1 (Greek) Narcissus is the flower of what goddess?

Q2 (Central American) How was the Aztec god Huitzilopochtli born?

Q3 (North American) In the lore of the Algonquian and Ojibwa tribes Paguk is a moving what?

Q4 (Greek) What objects did the cyclops provide Zeus, Poseidon and Hades with?

Q5 (Norse) Jotunheim is the land of what species?

Q6 (African) What is Omumborombonga in the lore of the Damara people?

Q7 (Irish) The hero Cú Chulainn is associated with what region of Ireland?

Q8 (Greek) What animal did Hera turn the river nymph Io into?

Q9 (Irish) What did the second wife of the sea god Lir, Aoife, turn her four step children into?

Q10 (Greek) Who is the god of the Greek underworld?

Expert 1

Q1 (Mongolian) The creator god Qormusta Tengri created humans from what three things?

Q2 (West Indies) In the lore of the Taino, what emerged from the cave Giovava?

Q3 (South American) Epunamun is a supreme god or war god of what people?

Q4 (African) The Fon god of destiny, Fa, is said to have how many eyes?

Q5 (Greek) What island was the goddess Circe exiled to?

Q6 (Hindu) What forest did the fire god Agni consume as a result of his insatiable appetite?

Q7 (Persian) How was the primeval man Gayomart created?

Q8 (Pacific Islands) What is the Polynesian fisherman Yusup best known for catching?

Q9 (Siberian) The rain god Abakan Khan is khan of what river?

Q10 (Norse) The frost giant Thiassi coveted what goddess of youth?

Expert 2

Q1 (Japanese) Hotei is a god of what?

Q2 (Arabian) The prophet Khadir became immortal after drinking from what?

Q3 (Greek) Electra's tears turned into drops of what?

Q4 (European) How does the forest spirit Ovda kill people?

Q5 (Central American) What is the name of the refuge from which the Aztec people emerged?

Q6 (South American) Who was the first mortal in the lore of the Incas?

Q7 (Japanese) What object was used to persuade the Shinto sun goddess Amaterasu to come out of her cave?

Q8 (North American) What did the Algonquin wolf god Malsum use to kill his brother?

Q9 (African) Ruwa is a supreme god of what people?

Q10 (Norse) What is the goddess Frigga's palace called?

Expert 3

Q1 (British) The monk Nennius is best known for what work?

Q2 (Mesopotamian) The warrior Enkidu was created by the goddess Aruru from what two ingredients?

Q3 (North American) Qagwaai is a monster in the form of what?

Q4 (European) What object is Olivant in the legends of Charlemagne?

Q5 (Japanese) The Shinto underworld, Yomi-tsu-kuni, is said to have how many regions?

Q6 (Pacific Islands) The Tongan wind god Laufakanaa is credited with inventing what?

Q7 (North American) The guardian spirit of the Karok tribe, Aikiren, lives on top of what mountain?

Q8 (North American) The wind god of the Wintun tribe, Kahit, is depicted as what animal?

Q9 (African) In Kenyan lore, how is a rainbow associated with the Rainbow Monster?

Q10 (Irish) Airbedruad refers to an impenetrable what?

Expert 4

Q1 (New Zealand) The Maori god Rona fights perpetually with what?

Q2 (Hindu) Agrasandhari is a book of what?

Q3 (Roman) Who is said to have been the sixth King of Rome?

Q4 (North American) According to the lore of the Haida people, how did the creator god Raven cause the earth to rise from the primeval ocean?

Q5 (Arabian) Mount Qaf is said to be made of what?

Q6 (Greek) What service does Hebe provide to the gods?

Q7 (South American) What was Guayacan in the lore of the Incas?

Q8 (Japanese) Shichi Fukujin are the seven Shinto deities of what?

Q9 (Hindu) The fire god Agni is depicted as having how many tongues?

Q10 (Pacific Islands) Loa is the creator god of what islands?

Expert 5

Q1 (Inuit) What three things did Anguta create?

Q2 (Hindu) What term refers to the first age of the world?

Q3 (Norse) Sigmund was the only person who could pull the sword Gram out of what oak tree?

Q4 (Greek) How many heads does the dragon Ladon have?

Q5 (Central American) In Aztec lore Falling Eagle was one of how many giants who supported the sky at the beginning of the Fifth Sun?

Q6 (Pacific Islands) The hero Budda of Infinite Light was born after what impregnated a woman?

Q7 (North American) What did the creator god of the Salish people, Amotken, create from hairs off his head?

Q8 (Hebrew) What did the demon Sakhar steal from King Solomon?

Q9 (African) The supreme god of the Banyarwanda people, Imana, created the world in how many layers?

Q10 (Norse) What is the name of the god Odin's spear?

Expert 6

Q1 (British) On what legendary island was the sword Excalibur forged?

Q2 (Korean) The king of Gamag Nara sends out Fire Dogs in fruitless attempts to capture what?

Q3 (Mesopotamian) How many other gods were born with the god Teshub?

Q4 (Japanese) Jui Chu is a pearl with the power to do what?

Q5 (Norse) The home of the good elves, Alfheim, is positioned between what two places?

Q6 (Greek) Nike is the goddess of what?

Q7 (Central American) Who is the Aztec god of agriculture?

Q8 (British) *Courser* was the ship of what sailor hero?

Q9 (North American) Where did the Iroquois earth goddess, Ataensic, fall from?

Q10 (Norse) Dwales-doll is a name for the sun used by what race?

Expert 7

Q1 (Japanese) Fukuro was an owl which became a what?

Q2 (North American) Ahsonnutli is the creator god of what tribe?

Q3 (Norse) *Skidbladnir* is the ship of what god?

Q4 (Greek) What was the name of the daughter Agamemnon sacrificed during the Trojan War?

Q5 (Greek) Symplegades refers to rocks at the entrance to what sea?

Q6 (Central American) In Aztec lore, what sun god is the twin brother of Quetzalcoatl?

Q7 (British) Which Knight of the Round Table killed the monster Addanc?

Q8 (Japanese) What does the god of marriage Gekka-O use to bind the feet of lovers together?

Q9 (Pacific Islands) The Pilipino deity Lumawig created humans from what?

Q10 (Chinese) I-mu-kuo is a mythical land where people have only one eye. Where is the eye positioned?

Expert 8

Q1 (Inuit) What is the Inuit spirit of the hunt?

Q2 (Roman) The fertility god Picus was turned into what type of bird?

Q3 (Greek) What did the King of Argos, Tantalus, famously do to his son?

Q4 (New Zealand) What happened as a result of the god Tane forcing his parents apart?

Q5 (European) The demon Aim is depicted with three heads. What animals are each of the heads?

Q6 (Central American) Nemontemi refers to how many unlucky days at the end of the Mayan calendar year?

Q7 (British) The Knight of the Round Table Epinogrus was the son of the King of what?

Q8 (Japanese) The Shinto thunder god Aji-Shiki-Taka-Hiko-Ne made so much noise as a child that he was condemned to what?

Q9 (Egyptian) What part of the dead does the goddess Selket guard?

Q10 (Norse) Ask, the first man created by Odin, was made from what?

Expert 9

Q1 (British) What castle was the home of King Pelles?

Q2 (Hindu) What name was given to the continent situated at the centre of the world?

Q3 (Japanese) Yellow Dragon is said to have emerged from what river?

Q4 (Greek) After the warrior-hero Ajax died, what is said to have sprung up where his blood stained the ground?

Q5 (Egyptian) Besides from the four quarters of the Earth, what else do the Sons of Horus guard?

Q6 (Mesopotamian) What is the storm god Adad depicted wearing?

Q7 (Pacific Islands) Damura is compared to a figure from what Western fairytale?

Q8 (North American) Why was the Iowa god Ictinike expelled from Heaven?

Q9 (Chinese) What does the deity Hun-tun represent?

Q10 (Australian) How did the creator god First Ancestor turn his first creations – tiny black lizards – into human beings?

Expert 10

Q1 (Hindu) Bhima is the hero of what epic?

Q2 (British) What was the king Twrch Trwyth transformed into as a punishment for his sins?

Q3 (Japanese) What is the Shinto wind god Fujin depicted wearing?

Q4 (Roman) Horatii refers to how many brothers?

Q5 (Pacific Islands) Aluluei is a god of what?

Q6 (North American) Blue World is the second of how many worlds the Navaho passed through before emerging into the upper world?

Q7 (North American) In the lore of the Yurok, Pulekekwerek is known for doing what?

Q8 (Chinese) Name the Eight Fairies, which were revered as controllers of the universe.

Q9 (African) Who is the supreme god of the Yaunde people?

Q10 (Australian) The spirit snake Bobbi-bobbi is said to have created the boomerang from what?

Expert 11

Q1 (Irish) The Fianna served as the bodyguard to the king of what?

Q2 (Arabian) What name is given to the green horses said to live in the Indian Ocean?

Q3 (Greek) Who was Achilles's father?

Q4 (European) What is Epona the goddess of in Gaul?

Q5 (Central American) Etzalqualiztli is an Aztec festival, celebrated in honour of what god?

Q6 (Greek) Phaenon, the first man, was made from clay by who?

Q7 (Egyptian) What is the king Koftarim said to have built?

Q8 (Greek) Who gave Theseus a ball of magic twine that enabled him to escape the Labyrinth after he had killed the Minotaur?

Q9 (Greek) Who was given three golden apples by Aphrodite?

Q10 (European) Elf-locks are tangles in the hair of what animal?

Expert 12

Q1 (Irish) How did the wise old fish, the Salmon of Knowledge acquire its intelligence?

Q2 (Greek) Achates was a friend of what Trojan hero?

Q3 (Greek) The King of Pherae, Admetus, took part in the hunt for what monster?

Q4 (European) On what two dates is the Celtic festival of Samhain celebrated?

Q5 (Central American) What Mayan god was thought to swallow the sun during eclipses?

Q6 (Greek) Pandora's box was given to Pandora as a gift when she married who?

Q7 (South American) In the lore of the Yahgan people, what was the only vulnerable part of the Stone Giant's anatomy?

Q8 (Greek) What type of creature is Euryale?

Q9 (Central American) Ah Punch is the Mayan god of what?

Q10 (Central American) How are the Saiyamkoob – Mayan dwarfs – fed?

Answers

Easy 1

Q1 Wealth
Q2 Underworld
Q3 Sun Sister
Q4 4
Q5 Venus
Q6 West
Q7 Wine
Q8 Creation
Q9 Flood
Q10 Chickasaw

Easy 2

Q1 Sioux
Q2 Dragon
Q3 Locusts
Q4 Bell
Q5 Wings
Q6 Odin
Q7 Immortality
Q8 Sailor
Q9 Giants
Q10 Youth

Easy 3

Q1 Homer
Q2 Epic poem
Q3 Death
Q4 Sky
Q5 Wolf
Q6 Cat
Q7 Mars
Q8 Hammer

Q9 Gold
Q10 Snakes

Easy 4

Q1 Zeus
Q2 3
Q3 Jewel
Q4 Darkness
Q5 Dwarfs
Q6 Vortigern
Q7 Green
Q8 Love
Q9 Mount Fuji
Q10 Speech

Easy 5

Q1 Tatars
Q2 Gawain
Q3 Sword
Q4 Soul
Q5 *Argo*
Q6 Architect
Q7 Square
Q8 A stone
Q9 Tears
Q10 The sea

Easy 6

Q1 Apollo
Q2 Chariot
Q3 Derbyshire
Q4 Metalwork
Q5 Clay
Q6 The moon

Q7 Stag
Q8 Wine
Q9 Every 8 years
Q10 Pebble

Easy 7

Q1 London
Q2 6
Q3 Palm trees
Q4 Language
Q5 Food and drink
Q6 Second Sun
Q7 Monks
Q8 Phoenix
Q9 Father
Q10 Hearts

Easy 8

Q1 Willow
Q2 21,000
Q3 Life
Q4 Fire
Q5 The alphabet
Q6 Muses
Q7 Camelot
Q8 Scotland
Q9 Nile
Q10 Brass

Easy 9

Q1 Sang
Q2 Drowned seamen
Q3 Brother
Q4 4

Q5 Thebes
Q6 Prophecy
Q7 Sword
Q8 Serpent
Q9 Eagle
Q10 Warriors

Easy 10

Q1 Finland
Q2 Sun
Q3 King
Q4 Black
Q5 Centipede
Q6 Isis
Q7 Crops fail
Q8 Emu
Q9 Mischief
Q10 Ferryman

Easy 11

Q1 Eel
Q2 Shouted at it
Q3 Heel
Q4 Hoist the white sail to signal success
Q5 St George
Q6 3
Q7 Diamond Jousts
Q8 Berkshire
Q9 Merman
Q10 A flood

Easy 12

Q1 Harp
Q2 Lamp

Q3 Trojan War
Q4 Love
Q5 The sun
Q6 A mirror
Q7 Rock
Q8 Apollo
Q9 The seas
Q10 Hieroglyphics

Average 1

Q1 Egg
Q2 Fire
Q3 *Arabian Nights' Entertainments*
Q4 Hercules
Q5 Gods
Q6 The dead
Q7 Sea monster
Q8 Ra
Q9 Niger River
Q10 Theseus

Average 2

Q1 Papa
Q2 Mayan
Q3 Left
Q4 2
Q5 Dog
Q6 Athena
Q7 Centaurs
Q8 Hidden gold
Q9 Guinevere
Q10 Her brother, Manco Capac

Average 3

Q1 Right
Q2 Geoffrey of Monmouth
Q3 Man and goat
Q4 The end of the world
Q5 Cretan Bull
Q6 Olympus
Q7 Franks and Moors
Q8 Jesus
Q9 Jackal
Q10 Memphis

Average 4

Q1 Aztecs
Q2 North-east
Q3 Round Table
Q4 Apollo
Q5 Uranus
Q6 The underworld
Q7 Holy Lance
Q8 Ireland
Q9 Viracocha
Q10 Forehead

Average 5

Q1 Siblings
Q2 The Fisher King
Q3 Poison food
Q4 Inti
Q5 Ali Baba
Q6 Grand Canyon
Q7 Grendel
Q8 Icarus

Q9 Slovenes

Q10 Iceland

Average 6

Q1 Lancelot

Q2 Drink

Q3 Hera

Q4 Honey

Q5 Metalwork

Q6 The Grail quest

Q7 Nut

Q8 The sun

Q9 The sea

Q10 Eagle

Average 7

Q1 Solomon

Q2 Inca

Q3 Brahma

Q4 Carpentry

Q5 Alexander the Great

Q6 Music

Q7 Mictlan

Q8 Merlin

Q9 River Nile

Q10 Rome

Average 8

Q1 Tlaloc

Q2 Bad souls of the deceased

Q3 Set

Q4 Taoism

Q5 Hunting

Q6 Eyes

Q7 Vishnu
Q8 Vulture
Q9 Persian Gulf
Q10 Fiji

Average 9

Q1 Fortune
Q2 Romulus and Remus
Q3 Warriors
Q4 Phoenix
Q5 Agriculture
Q6 Head
Q7 Armed and fully developed
Q8 Lyre
Q9 The Holy Grail
Q10 Craftsmen

Average 10

Q1 Baptism
Q2 Ugly
Q3 Prophecy
Q4 Leg
Q5 Carry the sky on his shoulders
Q6 Hermes
Q7 Treasure
Q8 Uther Pendragon
Q9 With the wheels of his chariot
Q10 Sea monster

Average 11

Q1 Water
Q2 Their wedding night
Q3 His own reflection
Q4 Mime

Q5 Lancelot
Q6 Aegeus
Q7 Heaven
Q8 Hindu
Q9 Ferryman
Q10 The Golden Fleece

Average 12

Q1 Aladdin
Q2 River Styx
Q3 Greeks and Trojans
Q4 The underworld
Q5 Prophecy
Q6 Mediterranean Sea
Q7 Face
Q8 Stones
Q9 The Lower Kingdom
Q10 Her twin brother, Geb

Average 13

Q1 Mother
Q2 It to come to life
Q3 Fire
Q4 Gold
Q5 Hawaii
Q6 Hunting
Q7 Knife
Q8 The underworld
Q9 The sun
Q10 Excrement

Average 14

Q1 Sister
Q2 Romulus and Remus

Q3 Sparta
Q4 Children
Q5 Fishermen
Q6 Earth-bearer
Q7 The world
Q8 India
Q9 They point both ways
Q10 Troy

Average 15

Q1 Sandals
Q2 Stone
Q3 Muses
Q4 10
Q5 Two corn seeds
Q6 Mountains
Q7 Immortals
Q8 Mountain
Q9 Marriage
Q10 From east to west

Average 16

Q1 The underworld
Q2 Earth
Q3 Coatlicue
Q4 Blackfoot tribe
Q5 Snake
Q6 Saliva of the gods
Q7 Love
Q8 Pretending madness
Q9 Thor
Q10 Cauldron

Average 17

Q1 Hercules
Q2 Uther
Q3 Chac
Q4 Unicorns
Q5 His children
Q6 The sun and the moon
Q7 Souls of the dead
Q8 Cyclops
Q9 Wolf
Q10 Amphitrite

Average 18

Q1 Sculptures
Q2 Climbed to the top of a mountain
Q3 Horse
Q4 War
Q5 Golden harp
Q6 Frigga
Q7 Sioux
Q8 Athena
Q9 Wisdom
Q10 Peleus

Average 19

Q1 Helen of Troy
Q2 Huitzilopochtli
Q3 The first man, Ouiot
Q4 One
Q5 Rope
Q6 Flaming sword
Q7 The Buddha
Q8 Flute

Q9 The moon
Q10 50

Average 20

Q1 Demeter
Q2 Fully formed and fully armed
Q3 Skeleton
Q4 Thunderbolt (Zeus), trident (Poseidon), helmet of invisibility (Hades)
Q5 Giants
Q6 A tree
Q7 Ulster
Q8 Cow
Q9 Swans
Q10 Hades

Expert 1

Q1 Fire, water and wind
Q2 The sun and the moon
Q3 Araucanian people
Q4 16
Q5 Aeaea
Q6 Khandava forest
Q7 With the sweat of Ahura Mazda
Q8 The magic white tortoise, Notu
Q9 Abakan River
Q10 Iduna

Expert 2

Q1 Laughter
Q2 The Well of Life
Q3 Amber
Q4 Tickling
Q5 Chicomoztoc

Q6 Guamansuri
Q7 Mirror
Q8 An owl feather
Q9 Chagga people
Q10 Fensalir

Expert 3

Q1 *Historia Brittonum*
Q2 Clay and spittle
Q3 Whale
Q4 Ivory horn
Q5 16
Q6 The fishing net
Q7 Sugarloaf Mountain
Q8 Bat
Q9 Its reflection
Q10 Magic hedge

Expert 4

Q1 The moon
Q2 Judgement
Q3 Servius Tullius
Q4 By flapping his wings
Q5 Emerald
Q6 Cupbearer
Q7 A primordial lake
Q8 Good fortune
Q9 7
Q10 Marshall Islands

Expert 5

Q1 The earth, sea and sky
Q2 Krita-yuga
Q3 Barnstokkr

Q4 100
Q5 4
Q6 The sun
Q7 Five goddesses
Q8 A magic ring
Q9 3
Q10 Gungnir

Expert 6

Q1 Avalon
Q2 The sun or moon
Q3 2
Q4 Make every wish come true
Q5 Heaven and Earth
Q6 Victory
Q7 Xipe Totec
Q8 Stormalong
Q9 Heaven
Q10 Dwarfs

Expert 7

Q1 Monk
Q2 Navajo
Q3 Frey
Q4 Iphigenia
Q5 Black Sea
Q6 Xolotl
Q7 Peredur
Q8 Fine red silk thread
Q9 Reeds
Q10 Forehead

Expert 8

Q1 Aglookik

Q2 Woodpecker

Q3 Served him in a stew

Q4 Raised the sky above the Earth

Q5 Human, cat and snake

Q6 5

Q7 Northumberland

Q8 Sit on a boat that eternally sails around the islands of Japan

Q9 Entrails

Q10 Ash tree

Expert 9

Q1 Castle Carbonek

Q2 Jambridvipa

Q3 Lo River

Q4 Hyacinth

Q5 The organs of the deceased

Q6 A horned headdress

Q7 Cinderella

Q8 For trickery

Q9 Chaos

Q10 By cutting off their tails

Expert 10

Q1 *Mahabharata*

Q2 A boar

Q3 Leopard skin

Q4 3

Q5 Navigation

Q6 4

Q7 Monster-slaying

Q8 Earth, Moon, Seasons, Sky, Sun, War, Yang and Yin

Q9 Zamba
Q10 One of his ribs

Expert 11

Q1 Ulster
Q2 Farasi Bahari
Q3 King Peleus of Phthia
Q4 Horsemen
Q5 The rain god, Tlaloc
Q6 Prometheus
Q7 The Pharos lighthouse (Alexandria)
Q8 Ariadne
Q9 Hippomenes
Q10 Horse

Expert 12

Q1 The Nuts of Knowledge
Q2 Aeneas
Q3 Calydonian Boar
Q4 31st October and 1st November
Q5 Ah Ciliz
Q6 Epimetheus
Q7 Soles of his feet
Q8 Gorgon
Q9 Death
Q10 With a pipeline from Heaven

Also by B.R. Egginton

Non-Fiction

Shorthand SOS: Learn Teeline Shorthand FAST

Richard II: The Tyranny of the White Hart (History Crash Courses)

Henry Hotze: The Master of Confederate Diplomacy

CV and Cover Letter Crash Course

The Ultimate History Quiz

The Ultimate French Monarchs Quiz

The Ultimate British Royal Navy Quiz

The Ultimate English Monarchs Quiz

The Ultimate British Primes Ministers Quiz

The Ultimate U.S. Presidents Quiz

NHL 2018-19 Season Quiz

Fiction

A Kingdom of Our Own

The Sixth Number (Parts 1-3)

The Chronicles of Ascension (Novellas 1-6)

History Quest: The Plot (Episode I)

Printed in Poland
by Amazon Fulfillment
Poland Sp. z o.o., Wrocław

53892318R00049